GARY LLOYD NOLAND

COLLECTED PIANO WORKS
VOLUME 1

7TH SPECIES PUBLICATIONS

13080 Princeton Court, Lake Oswego OR 97035

email: nolandgary5@gmail.com
website: https://composergarynoland.godaddysites.com/

Published by 7th Species
13080 Princeton Court
Lake Oswego OR 97035

Composer's website: https://composergarynoland.godaddysites.com/

Contact email: nolandgary5@gmail.com

ISMN: 979-0-58094-001-8 • ISBN/SKU: 978-1-7323023-8-9
EISBN: 978-1-0879-7629-7

First printed 2021

Title page illustration by Lon Gaylord Dylan (the composer's visual artist alter ego); see Composer's Notes for detailed information on book's interior score cover illustrations

Cover photo of Gary Lloyd Noland taken by composer Greg Steinke at the Ernest Bloch Music Festival in Newport, Oregon, Summer 1994

Cover design by Maduranga Thebuwana

Cover photo for VENGE ART Fascicle #5 excerpt taken by the composer in Anacapri, atop the Isle of Capri (September, 1999)

Also by GARY LLOYD NOLAND

Books
(written under pen name Dolly Gray Landon)

JAGDLIED: a Chamber Novel for Narrator, Musicians, Pantomimists, Dancers & Culinary Artists

NOTHING IS MORE: a High Black Comedy in Verse with Music for Six Actors

Music CDs

Available from NorthPacificMusic.com:

SELECTED MUSIC FROM VENGE ART
ROYAL OILWORKS MUSIC
24 INTERLUDES FOR PIANO OP. 71, VOL. 1
24 INTERLUDES FOR PIANO OP. 71, VOL. 2
24 POSTLUDES FOR PIANO OP. 72, VOL. 1
24 POSTLUDES FOR PIANO OP. 72, VOL. 2

in collaboration with other composers:

PASSION
PLAYERLESS PIANOS

Available from 7th Species (https://composergarynoland.godaddysites.com/)

20 COVIDITTIES OP. 116 (double CD)
ENTROPIC ABANDON (double CD)
MUSIC OF RAGE, SORROW, LOVE, LAUGHTER & BUREAUCRACY (double CD, release pending)
DISSONAPHOBIC FEVER DREAMS Op. 118
STATE-OF-THE-ART EAR EXERCISES FOR MUSICAL COGNOSCENTI Op. 119
WAYWARD AFFECTS & AFFLICTIONS Op. 120

MUSIC SCORES

Multiple items available from Freeland (7th Species) Publications, J.W. Pepper, Sheet Music Plus, RGM

COMPOSER'S NOTES

ENIGMOUS PRELUDE Op. 103 (2019) is dedicated to Belgian pianist Lukas Huisman. Cover illustration by the composer's alter ego, Lon Gaylord Dylan.

SCHIZOMEZZO Op. 85 (2006) is dedicated to British composer/pianist Michael Finnissy and was premiered by pianist Maria Choban on March 18th, 2011 at Lincoln Hall, Portland State University. Her performance can be heard at the following link: https://cascadiacomposers.org/wp-content/uploads/2011/03/Noland.mp3. A studio recording was later made by M. Choban, which is available on the double CD ENTROPIC ABANDON: https://www.amazon.com/ENTROPIC-ABANDON-Super-Psychedelic-Decadissident-Flextravabonanza/dp/B08VXC9X5S. Aforesaid recording may be heard at the following link: https://soundcloud.com/gary-noland/schizomezzo-for-piano-op-85

MORTESQUE Op. 31 (1993) was composed in memory of composer Stephen Albert after he died in an automobile accident in December, 1992. Cover illustration by Lon Gaylord Dylan.

PRELUDE IN E MINOR for piano or harpsichord Op. 34 (1979, revised 1993) is available on the ROYAL OILWORKS MUSIC CD and can be heard here: https://soundcloud.com/gary-noland/prelude-in-e-minor-for-harpsichord-op-34. Cover illustration by Lon Gaylord Dylan.

RAGBONES Op. 11 (1988) was premiered on December 4th, 1988 by pianist Mark Lutton at Paine Hall, Harvard University. It is available on the ROYAL OILWORKS MUSIC CD and can be heard here: https://soundcloud.com/gary-noland/ragbones-for-piano-op-11. Ragbones was also performed by pianist Inga van Buren on Jan. 25th, 2014 at a house concert at the home of Sylvia Gray and Viktors Berstis in Portland, Oregon. Her performance can be accessed on the composer's YouTube channel. Cover illustration by Lon Gaylord Dylan.

GRIMPROVISATION Op. 38 was composed on New Year's Day, 1994. It was premiered by the composer on Jan. 22nd, 1995 on a Seventh Species concert at Western Oregon University in Monmouth, Oregon. Cover illustration by Lon Gaylord Dylan.

DEFORMED FUGUE Op. 17 (1977, revised 1990) was premiered by pianist Stephen Olsen at SICPP (Summer Institute for Contemporary Performance Practice) at the New England Conservatory in Boston on June 24th, 2006. When the concert was over Noland found the score of his fugue discarded on the floor, crumpled up and torn to shreds. This work may be performed on either harpsichord or piano. Listen here: https://soundcloud.com/gary-noland/deformed-fugue-for-harpsichord-op-17. Cover illustration by Lon Gaylord Dylan.

THREE PENITENTIAL EXCERCISES Op. 78 (misspelling intentional for arcane purposes, 2005) was premiered by the composer on October 15th, 2005 on a Seventh Species concert at Day Music Auditorium in Portland, Oregon. This performance is available for listening on YouTube.

ALLEGRO IN B FLAT MAJOR Op. 60 (1977, revised 2001) is the first movement of an unfinished piano sonata. The composer intends on revising the other movements at some point in the not-too-distant future, weather permitting.

EPICEDIUM Op. 58 (2001) was composed several weeks after the September eleventh, 2001 attacks on the World Trade Center and Pentagon as a memorial to the thousands of innocent victims who died that day. This piece was premiered by Noland's wife, Kaori Katayama, on a Seventh Species concert at Sherman Clay Recital Hall in the Pearl District of Portland, Oregon on November 10th, 2006. Here is a link to a performance of hers that took place at Beall Concert Hall at the University of Oregon School of Music in the Spring of 2007: https://soundcloud.com/gary-noland/epicedium-for-piano-op-58. This performance is slated for release on the double CD: MUSIC OF RAGE, SORROW, LOVE, LAUGHTER & BUREAUCRACY.

BLUES FLASH Op. 42 (1998) was premiered by pianist Ariel Borensztein on a 7th Species Concert at United Lutheran Church in Eugene, Oregon on November 17th, 1998. Consistent with its title, the cover was designed by LGD as a sort of cryptic homage to Monica Lewinsky.

ALLEMANDE IN F MAJOR Op. 76 for harpsichord or piano (1978, rev. 2005), in memory of Laurette Goldberg (1932-2005), Noland's harpsichord teacher in the late 1970s.

PRELUDE & ZOOTROT Op. 22 (1991) is dedicated to my wife Kaori Katayama and is available on the ROYAL OILWORKS MUSIC CD. It can be heard here: https://soundcloud.com/gary-noland/prelude-zootrot-for-piano-op-22. Cover illustration & design by Lon Gaylord Dylan.

FIVE PIECES FOR PIANO, VOLUME 2, Op. 41 (1998) was premiered by the composer on a Seventh Species concert at United Lutheran Church in Eugene, Oregon on October 27th, 1998. The fifth piece (Obsequy) was composed in memory of Ivan Tcherepnin (1943-1998).

LIEBESSCHMERZ FUGE (1981-2009) is dedicated to the memory of Lukas Foss (1922-2009). One can listen to this work at the following link: https://soundcloud.com/gary-noland/liebesschmerz-fuge-for-piano-op-95-2009. Cover illustration by Lon Gaylord Dylan.

FIVE PIECES FOR PIANO, VOLUME 1, Op. 40 (1998). Performances of the Aubade (No. 5) by pianists Anna Sutyagina and Ruta Kuzmickas are available on YouTube.

GELTSCHMERZ VALSE Op. 99 (2011) was premiered by pianist Jihye Chang on a Seventh Species concert at Michelle's Piano Company in Portland, Oregon on June 11th, 2013. Her performance can be accessed on the composer's YouTube channel or here: https://soundcloud.com/gary-noland/geltschmerz-valse-for-piano-op-99. This performance is slated for release on the double CD of Noland's compositions: MUSIC OF RAGE, SORROW, LOVE, LAUGHTER & BUREAUCRACY. Cover illustration by Lon Gaylord Dylan.

TWO-PART INVENTION IN D MAJOR Op. 81 (2006) was premiered at the Portland Piano International Festival by pianist Daniel Trang in 2012. Cover design and illustration by Lon Gaylord Dylan.

LOCOBRATIONS Op. 65 (2002) was premiered by pianist Paul Safar on a Seventh Species Concert at Colonial Heights Presbyterian Church on October 27th, 2012. His performance can be heard on the composer's YouTube channel or at the following link: https://soundcloud.com/gary-noland/locobrations-for-piano-op-65. Cover art by Lon Gaylord Dylan.

NERDFOX RAG (1978, revised 1991) was premiered by pianist Inga Van Buren at the Portland Piano International Festival in 2011. Her performance can be accessed on the composer's YouTube channel or one can listen to a mechanical rendition thereof here: https://soundcloud.com/gary-noland/nerdfox-rag-for-piano-op-23. Cover art by Lon Gaylord Dylan.

INVERTIVENTIONS Nos. 1 & 2 Op. 47 were composed in 2000 and 2002 respectively.

ADAGIETTO DOLOROSO Op. 121 (2021) was composed in memory of composer/pianist Frederic Rzewski (1938-2021). It may be heard here: https://soundcloud.com/gary-noland/adagietto-doloroso-in-g-minor-for-piano-in-memoriam-frederic-rzewski. Cover illustration and design by Lon Gaylord Dylan.

BROOM BRIGADE Op. 25 was premiered on a Seventh Species concert by the composer on November 11th, 1994 at Central Lutheran Church, Eugene, Oregon. Cover illustration by Lon Gaylord Dylan.

AETERNUM VALE Op. 93 (2008) was premiered by pianist Jihye Chang on a Seventh Species concert at Michelle's Piano Company in Portland, Oregon on June 11th, 2013. Her performance can be accessed on YouTube or at the following link: https://soundcloud.com/gary-noland/aeternum-vale-for-piano-op-93. This performance is slated for release on MUSIC OF RAGE, SORROW, LOVE, LAUGHTER & BUREAUCRACY. Cover art and design by Lon Gaylord Dylan.

ANDANTE IN F MINOR for piano four-hands Op. 46 (2000, revised 2002) was composed as an homage to Franz Schubert and was commissioned by pianist Mayumi Shigenaga and premiered by pianists Mayumi Shigenaga and Miho Ishida in Osaka, Japan on January 23, 2000. It has, since, been performed on several occasions by at least two other piano duos. Listen here: https://soundcloud.com/gary-noland/andante-in-f-minor-for-piano-four-hands-op-46.

THE MELANCHOLIC MONEYMONGER Op. 26 (1992) is dedicated to composer Ladislav Kupkovic (1936-2016). Cover illustration by Lon Gaylord Dylan.

TWO-PART INVENTION IN D MINOR Op. 70 (2006) was premiered at the Portland Piano International Festival by pianist Daniel Trang in 2012. The cover, while consisting primarily of clip art, is also illustrated and designed in part by Lon Gaylord Dylan.

FUNERAL WALTZ Op. 91 (2008) was composed in memory of John Swackhamer (1923-2006) and was premiered by pianist Ruta Kuzmickas on March 17th, 2013 on a Cascadia Composers concert at Colonial Heights Presbyterian Church in Portland, Oregon. Several of her performances of this piece can be accessed on the composer's YouTube channel. Here is a more recent rendition of the work (2020) by pianist Myrna Setiawan: https://soundcloud.com/gary-noland/pianist-myrna-setiawan-performs-funeral-waltz-op-91. M. Setiawan's rendition is slated for release on the double CD of Noland's compositions: MUSIC OF RAGE, SORROW, LOVE, LAUGHTER & BUREAUCRACY.

THREE LITTLE BONBONS Op. 59 (2001) is a set of three short pieces for children, which includes fingerings.

RUSSELL STREET RAG Op. 5 (1974-5, revised 2006) was premiered on December 4th, 1988 by pianist Mark Lutton at Paine Hall, Harvard University. A recording of Russell Street Rag was later made by pianist Randall Hodgkinson at the home of Paul Matisse (grandson of Henri Matisse and stepson of Marcel Duchamp) in Groton, MA, just outside of Boston, in November, 1987. R. Hodgkinson's performance was released by North Pacific Music on the CD recording SELECTED MUSIC FROM VENGE ART in 2002. R. Hodgkinson's performance can be heard here: https://soundcloud.com/gary-noland/russell-street-rag-for-piano-op-5. Pianist Inga van Buren's performance, which was featured on a Seventh Species concert at Sherman Clay Recital Hall in Portland on March 23rd, 2011, can be heard on the composer's website at: https://composergarynoland.godaddysites.com/music-videos-17. Cover illustration and design by Lon Gaylord Dylan.

VENGE ART FASCICLE #5 Op. 54 excerpt (2001) is one of multiple musical interludes interpolated into the 300,000-word text written by the composer's alter ego, author Dolly Gray Landon. Cover photo taken by the composer in Anacapri, atop the Isle of Capri (September, 1999).

TRIBUTE TO GARY NOLAND, COMPOSER

By what dim light,
Was I to expect—
Walking down those Berkeley paths,
When all I was told to believe was the
Grunt of weary nakedness buried beneath
The unenlightened night?
Anything . . .
By what dim light,
Was I to expect—
Passing further, south, by those musical mausoleums,
Built to accommodate our ears, our developing form of sense,
Into which they shoveled "hysterical, bleating wailing," and other
Mismatched drones of our times,
Was I to expect?
Anything . . .
And, too, remembering dry, aging lips at podiums, lecturing,
"The Iron Laws of Music History," their decade's long utterance of "Rosebud,"
While their former thugs—and other graduate gentry—unleashed,
Knocked the breath out of keyboards and tried
My ability to stay focused, while darting past.
Anything . . .
That was anything but the perceptive and deft notes
That arose as a sonic answer,
Innocent and infinitely powerful,
Filling a small studio tucked further south.
By what dim light,
Was I to expect—
Walking down those Berkeley paths,
Out of the stolid reach of the Berkeley campus:
the tonal nudity, and grace, of Gary Noland's work?

—JEFF BRITTING, American composer, playwright, author, and producer; Associate Producer and
Composer of the score of the academy-award nominated documentary: Ayn Rand: A Sense of Life
Poem © 2020 by Jeff Britting, West Hollywood

CONTENTS

Gary Lloyd Noland

Enigmous Prelude

for piano

Op. 103

for Lukas Huisman

Enigmous Prelude
for piano

Adagio
luminously morbid and severe

Gary Lloyd Noland, Op. 10.

GARY NOLAND
SCHIZOMEZZO
for piano

Op. 85

for Michael Finnissy

Schizomezzo

for piano

by Gary Noland, Op. 85 (2006

Andante tenebroso

♩ = ca. 82-86

First Edition: August, 2006

16

17

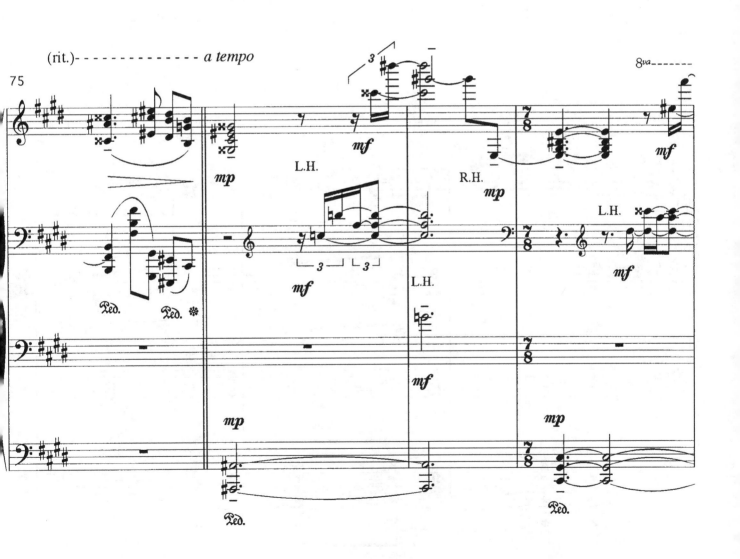

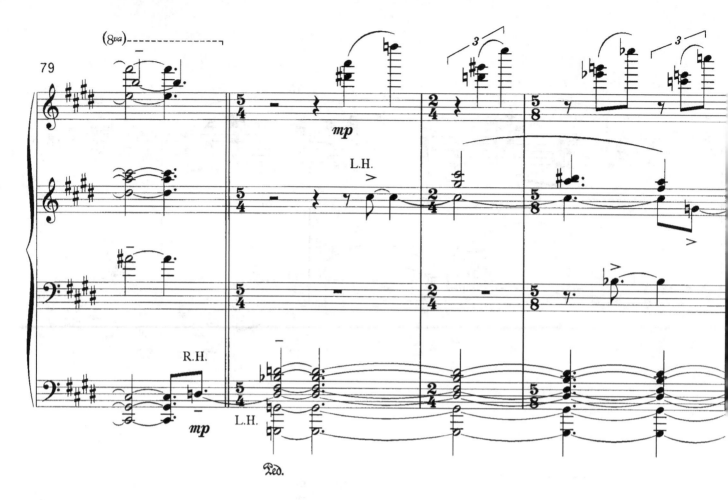

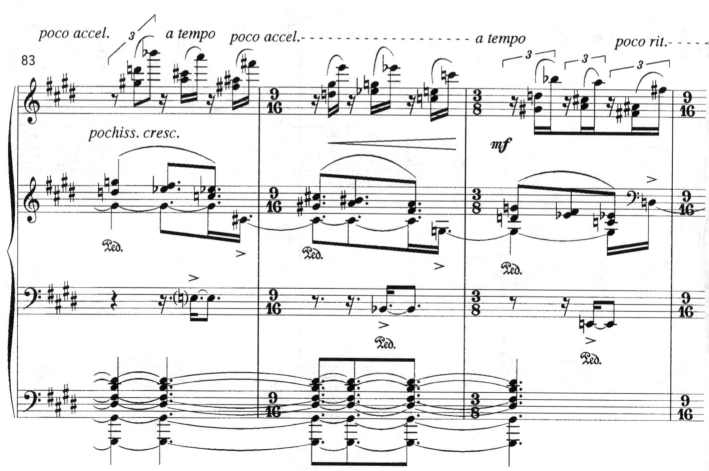

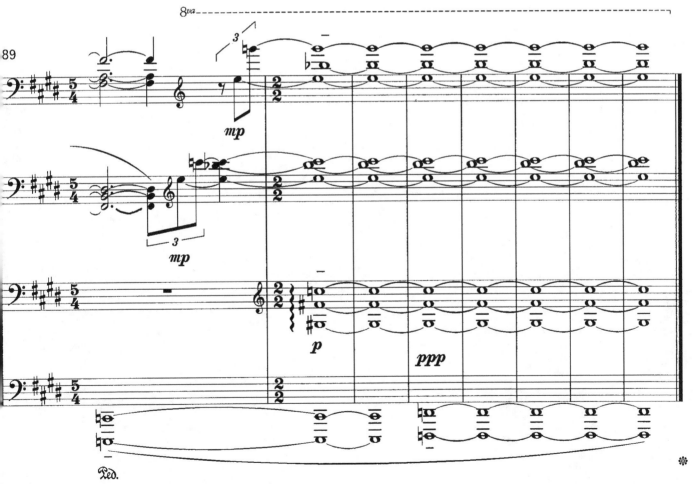

Gary Noland
Mortesque
for piano, Op. 31

"MORTESQUE"

for piano

by Gary Noland
Op. 31 (1993)

in memoriam Stephen Albert

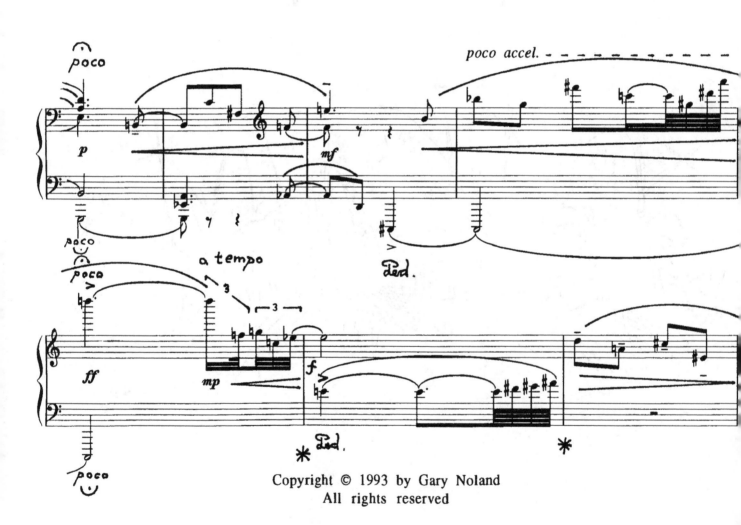

G. Noland
3/28/93
6:15 P.M.
Eugene, OR

Gary Noland
Prelude in E Minor
for harpsichord (or piano)
Op. 34

PRELUDE IN E MINOR
for Harpsichord (or Piano)

Gary Noland, Op. 34
(1979, revised 1993)

"Ragbones"

dedicated to Mark Lutton

for piano

composed 1977
revised 1988

Opus 11 by Gary Noland

Quite fast (♩ = ca. 72-86)

* F flat or F natural.

GARY NOLAND

GRIMPROVISATION
for piano

OP. 38

GRIMPROVISATION
for piano

Gary Noland, Op. 38

Adagietto espressivo

Deformed Fugue

for harpsichord (or piano)

by Gary Noland
Op. 17

dedicated to Emil Awad

FP17

GARY NOLAND

Three Penitential Excercises

for piano

Op. 78

Three Penitential Excercises for Piano
1. Sackcloth & Ashes

Austere

by Gary Noland, Op. 78, No. 1

♩ = ca. 42

2. Hair Shirt

by Gary Noland, Op. 78, No. 2

Humorless

♩ = ca. 72

59

3. Jock Strap

Andante

by Gary Noland, Op. 78, No. 3

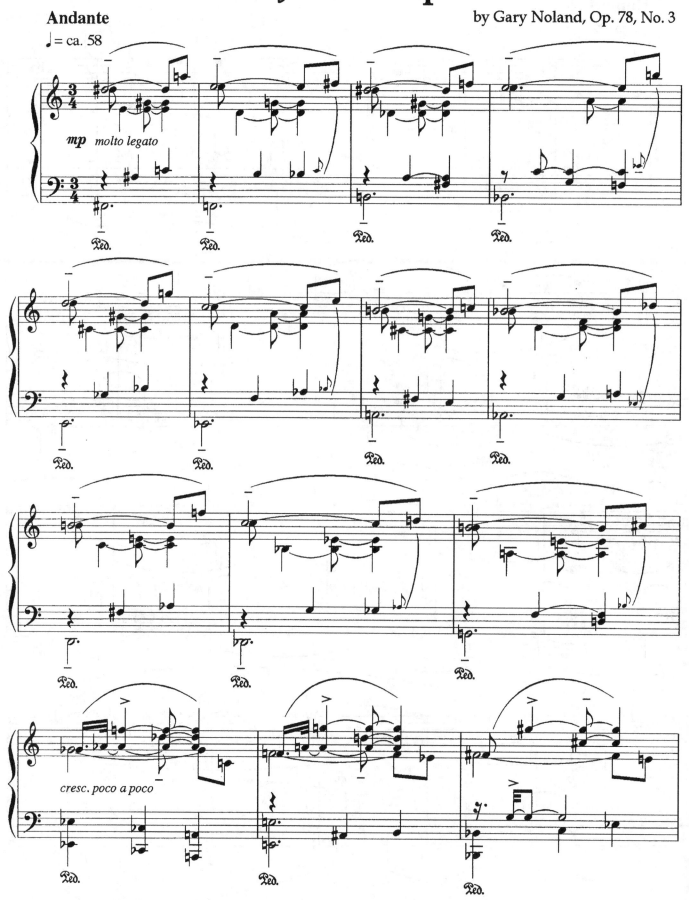

With machismo

ritardando poco a poco - - - - -

Adagio

61

GARY NOLAND

ALLEGRO

IN B FLAT MAJOR

for piano

Op. 60

Allegro in B Flat Major

for piano

Gary Noland, Op. 60
(1977, rev. 2001)

66

Tempo 1

GARY NOLAND

EPICEDIUM

for piano

in memory of the victims of the East Coast suicide attacks
September 11, 2001

Op. 58

EPICEDIUM
for piano

**in memory of the victims of the East Coast suicide attacks
September 11, 2001**

Gary Noland, Op. 58

Adagietto con gravità; molto espressivo

Hold final
sonority until it
fades into
silence.

GARY NOLAND

EXTRA! EXTRA! EXTRA! EXTRA! EXTRA!

BLUES FLASH
for piano

Op. 42

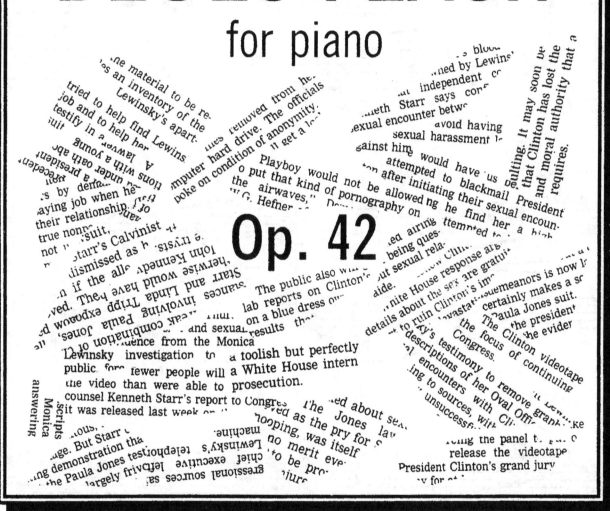

Blues Flash

for piano

Gary Noland, Op. 42

Andantino

Gary Noland

Allemande in F Major

for harpsichord or piano
Op. 76

in memoriam Laurette Goldberg

Allemande in F Major

for harpsichord or piano

by Gary Noland, Op. 76
(1978, rev. 2005)

*All trills begin on the upper auxiliary.

1. PRELUDE

for piano

dedicated to Kaori Katayama

by Gary Noland
Op. 22, no. 1

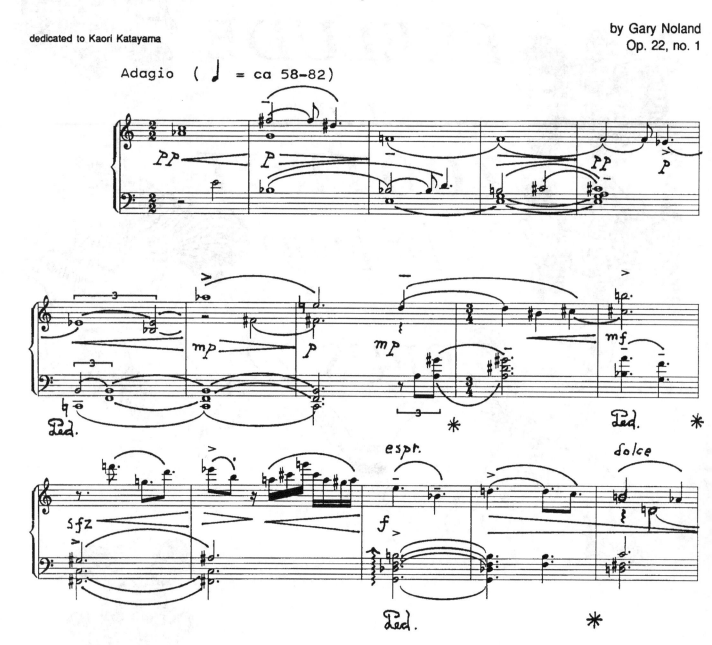

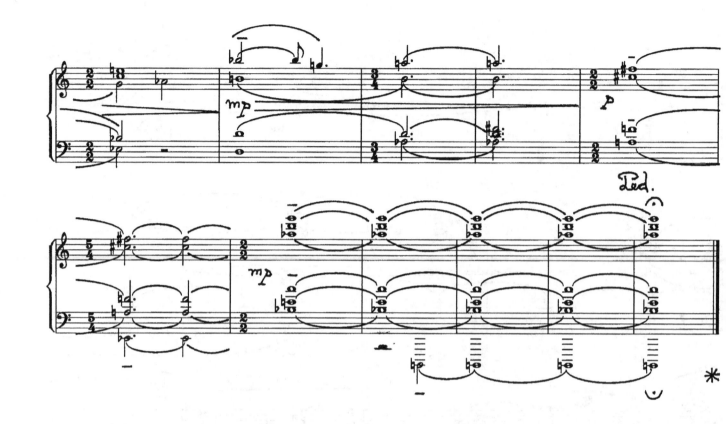

STAGE DIRECTIONS

A domesticated and/or exotic melange of quadruped and/or winged creatures (large and small) are to be released upon the stage directly prior to the performance of "Zootrot." The pianist has complete freedom of interpretation with regard to the species of animal(s) employed. The creatures chosen may either wander (or volitate) freely about the stage during the performance, or their movements may be monitored by skilled technicians for the purpose of producing a choreographic effect. Whatever means are employed should serve to complement rather than impede the interpretation of this work. (The composer, incidentally, can claim no responsibility for riotous pandemoniums that eventuate when technicians lose their whip hands over the beasts and fowls whereunto they've been appointed.)

2. ZOOTROT

for piano

dedicated to Kaori Katayama

by Gary Noland
Op. 22, no. 2

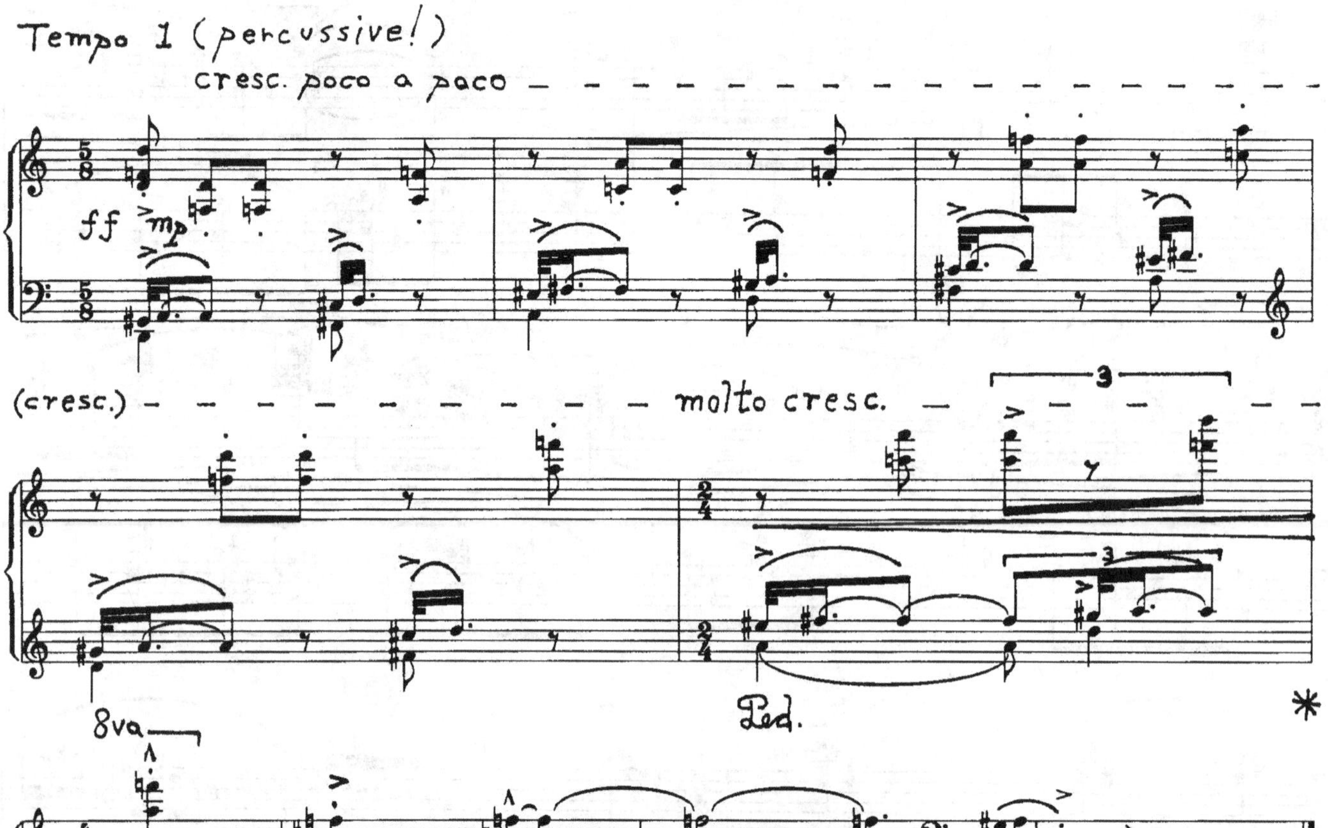
Tempo 1 (percussive!)
cresc. poco a poco
ff
mp
(cresc.)
molto cresc.
3
Ped.
8va
ff
f
Ped.
G. Noland, Berkeley, 12:17pm Sept. 14 1991

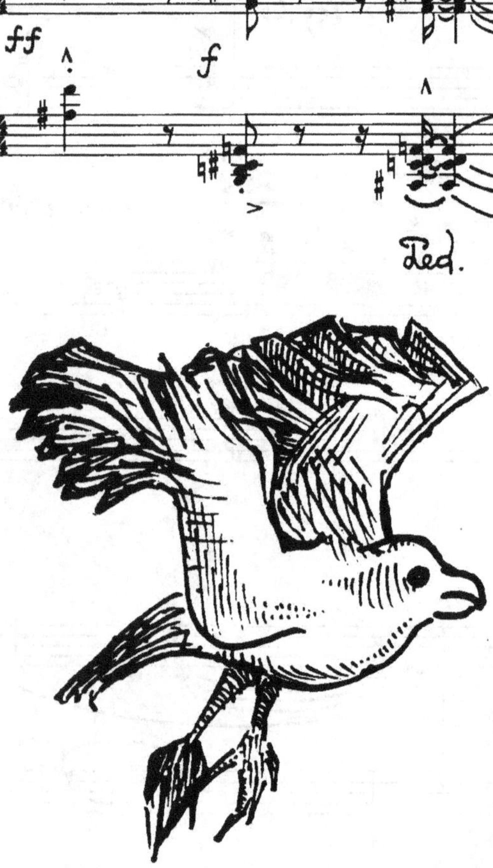

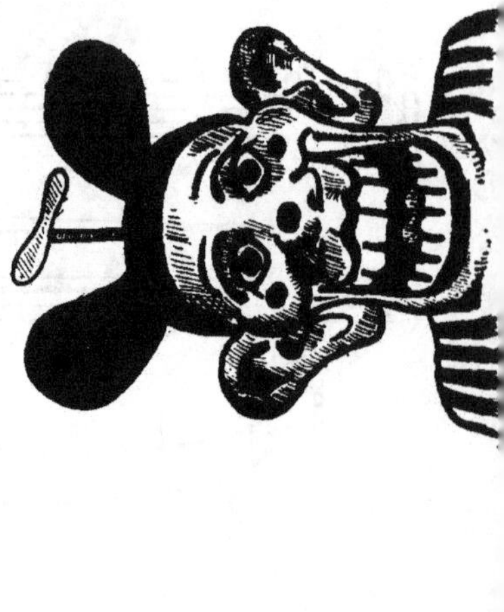

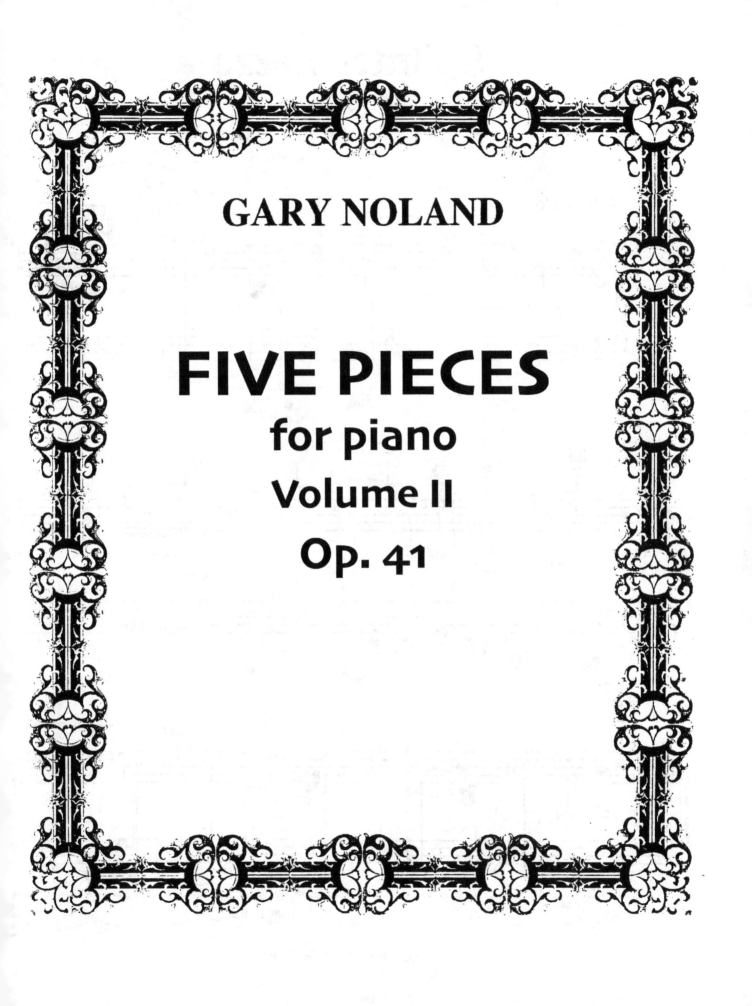

GARY NOLAND

FIVE PIECES
for piano
Volume II
Op. 41

Splintermezzo
for piano

Gary Noland, Op. 41, No. 1

Adagietto

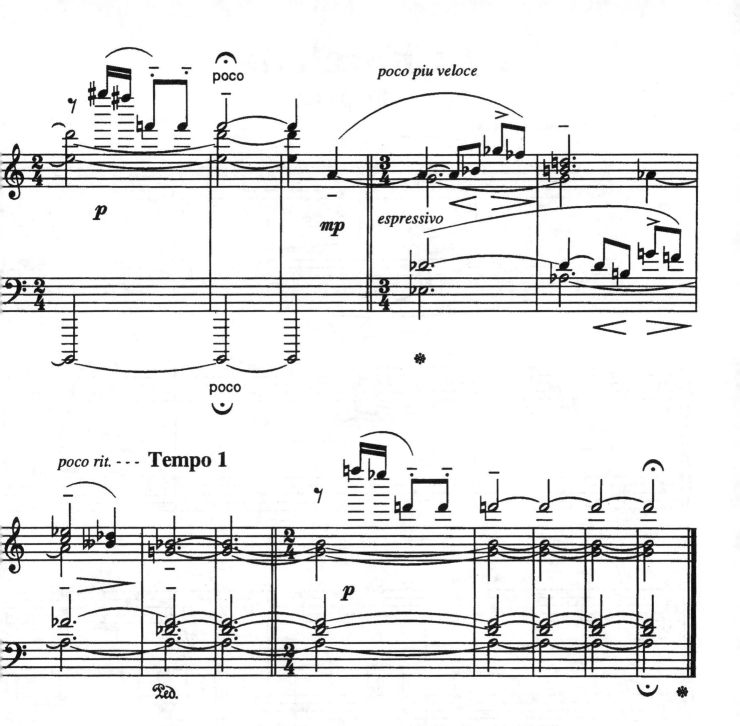

Choralude
for piano

Solemn and Severe

Gary Noland, Op. 41, No. 2

Zigzagatelle

Gary Noland, Op. 41, No. 3

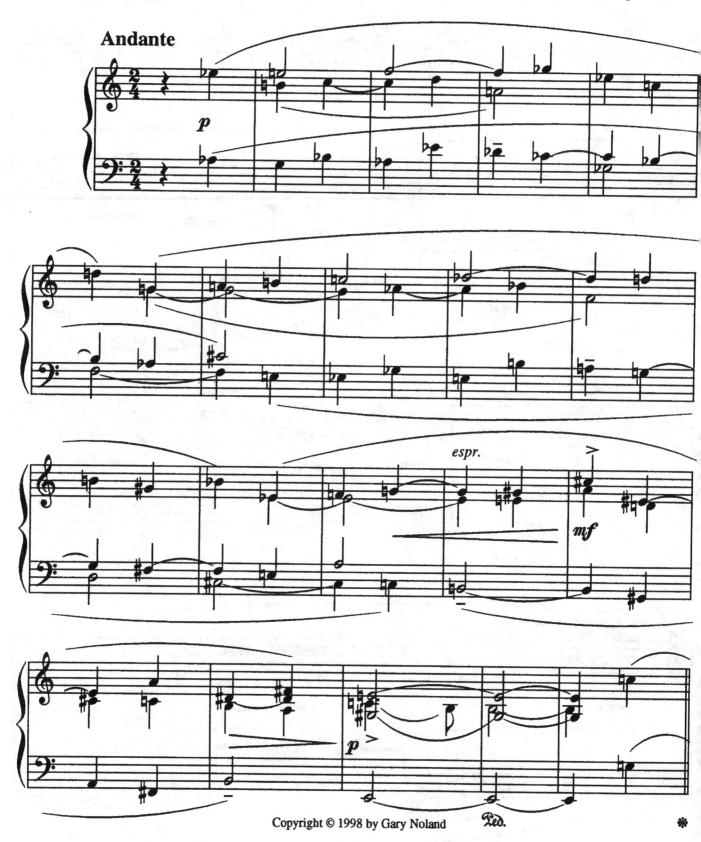

100

BLISSONANCE
for piano

Gary Noland, Op. 41, No.

Adagio

Obsequy
for piano

In memoriam Ivan Tcherepnin

Gary Noland, Op. 41, No. 5

Grave sostenuto

sempre *p* e con pedale

Ped.

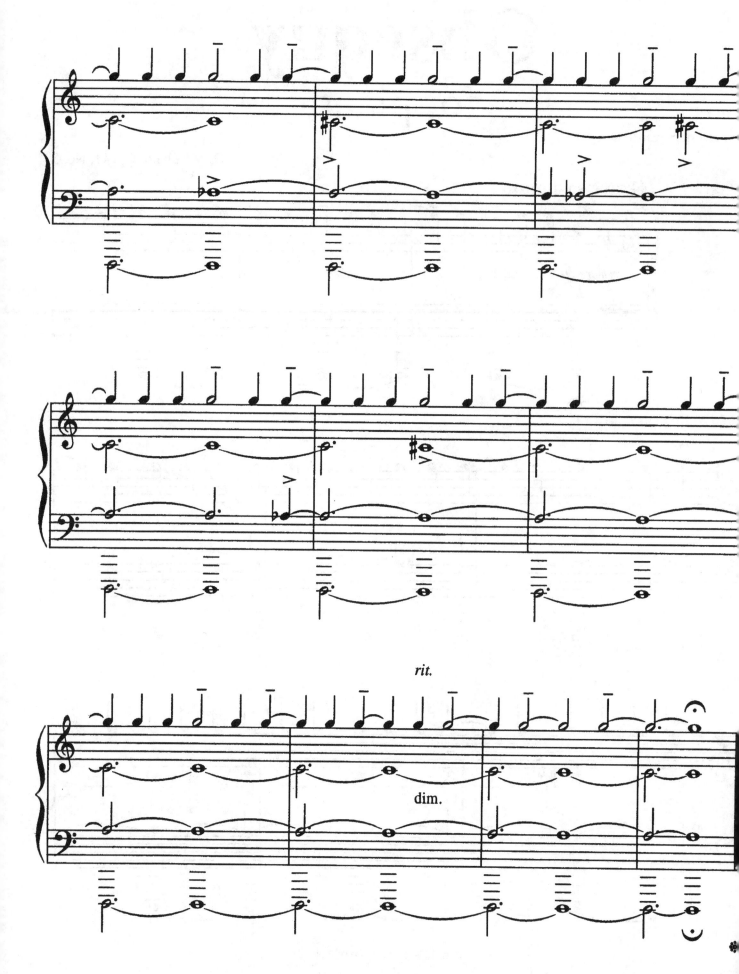

rit.

dim.

Gary Noland
Liebesschmerz Fuge
for piano
Op. 95

Liebesschmerz Fuge
in memoriam Lukas Foss
for piano

Allegro non troppo

by Gary Noland, Op. 95
(1981-2009)

* NB: All trills begin on the upper auxiliary.

114

mit angst

Intensify! - - - - - - - - - - - - - - - - - - con ostinazione

121

133

Luminoso

With grace and elegance

134

137

Andantino

pochiss. rit. -

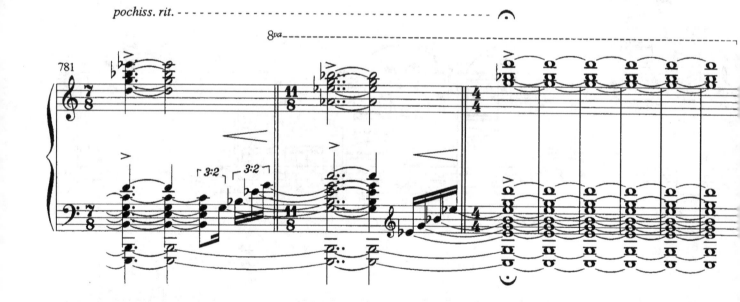

GARY NOLAND

Five Pieces
for piano
Volume I

Op. 40

Canonette in G Minor
for piano

Gary Noland, Op. 40, No. 1

Moderato

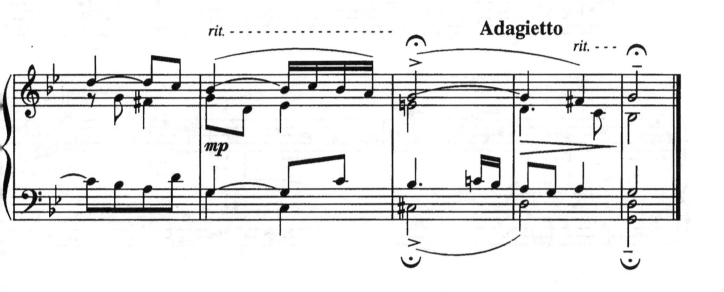

Berfelgunk
for piano

Gary Noland, Op. 40, No. 2

Moderato e Maestoso

*Begin trill on upper note.

144

Quodlibet
for piano

Gary Noland, Op. 40, No. 3

Moderato e Maestoso

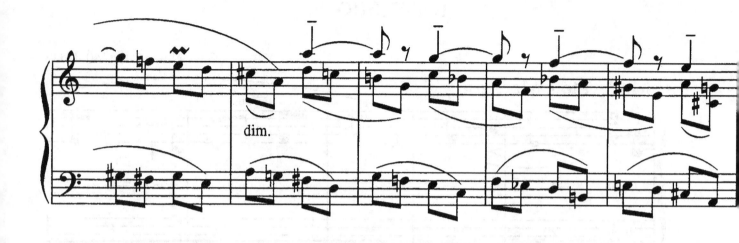

dim.

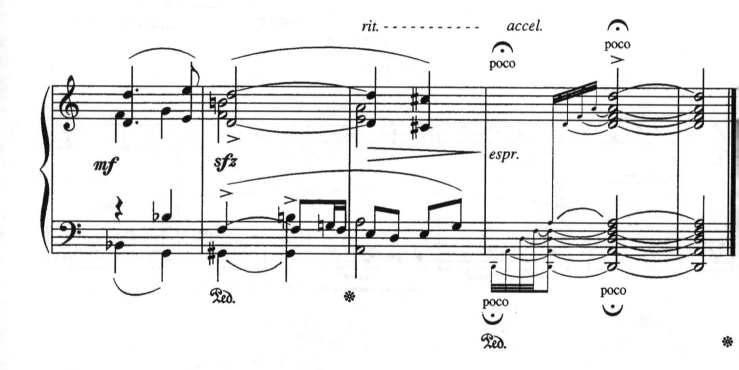

rit. - - - - - - - - - - - accel.

poco

poco

mf

sfz

espr.

poco

Ped.

poco

Ped.

146

Doris-Daylude

for piano

Gary Noland, Op. 40, No. 4

Allegretto giocoso

Aubade

for piano

Gary Noland, Op. 40, No.

Moderato cantabile

149

Gary Noland

GELTSCHMERZ VALSE

for piano

Op.99

FREELAND PUBLICATIONS

GELTSCHMERZ VALSE

for piano

by Gary Noland, Op. 99

Pensive; ennuyé

* inverted mordent

GARY NOLAND
TWO-PART INVENTION
in D Major
for Piano or Harpsichord

Op. 81

Freeland Publications
FP112

Two-Part Invention in D Major
for piano or harpsichord

by Gary Noland, Op. 81

NB: All trills begin on upper auxiliary.

for Joseph Fennimore

LOCOBRATIONS
for piano

Gary Noland, Op. 6

Largo Introspecto; molto rubato

Nerdfox Rag

for piano

by Gary Noland, op. 23
composed 1978; revised 1991

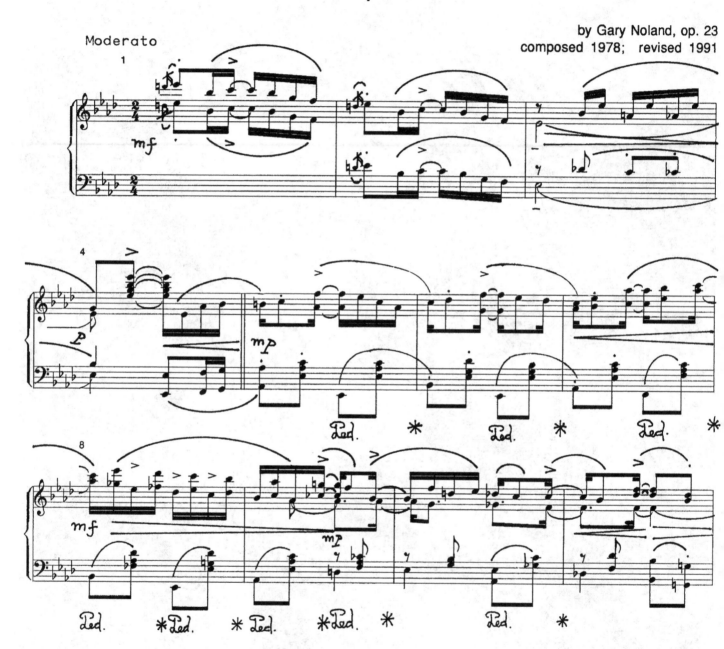

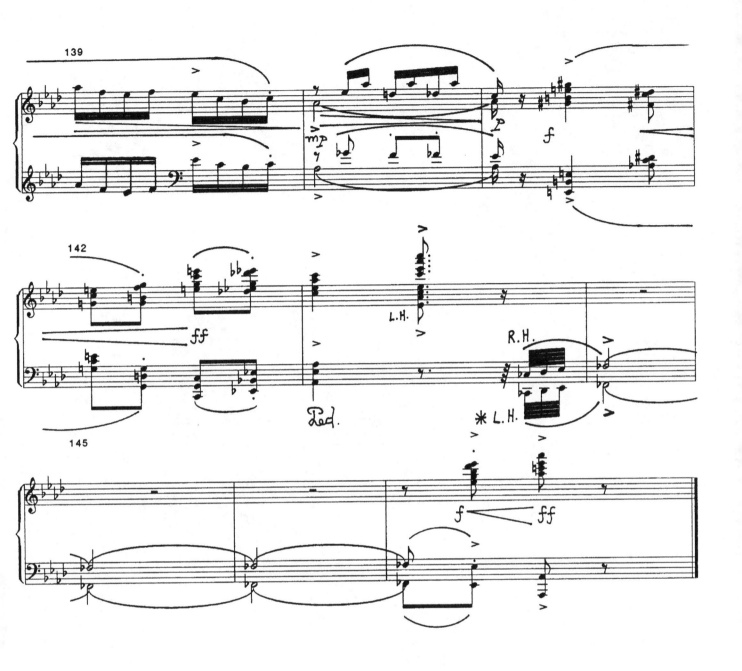

Gary Noland

Invertivention
No. 1
for piano

Op. 47, No. 1

FREELAND PUBLICATIONS
Fp 76

Invertivention No. 1
for piano

Gary Noland, Op. 47, No.

Moderato

*Trill begins on upper auxiliary.

Gary Noland

Invertivention No. 2

for piano

Op. 47, No. 2

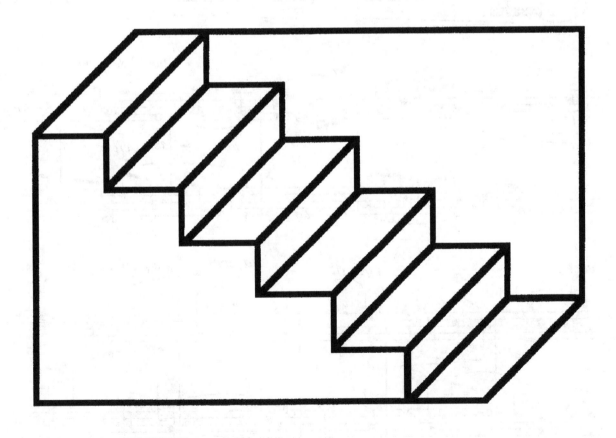

Freeland Publications
FP98

Invertivention No. 2
for piano

Gary Noland, Op. 47, No. 2

Moderato

*All trills begin on upper auxiliary.

GARY LLOYD NOLAND

ADAGIETTO DOLOROSO
for piano

Op. 121

In memoriam Frederic Rzewski
(1938-2021)

7th Species

Adagietto Doloroso

for piano

in memoriam Frederic Rzewski

by Gary Lloyd Noland, Op. 121

Adagietto doloroso

192

194

197

Gary Noland

The Broom Brigade

for piano, Op. 25

"The Broom Brigade"

for piano

by Gary Noland
Op. 25 (1992)

dedicated to Ivan Tcherepnin

Allegretto

FP 30

GARY NOLAND

AETERNUM VALE

for piano

Op. 93

Freeland Publications

FP125

AETERNUM VALE
in memoriam David Foster Wallace (1962-2008)
for piano

Gary Noland, Op. 93

Adagietto con accoramento

205

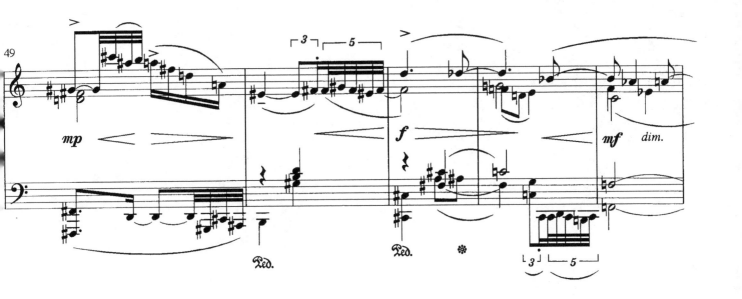

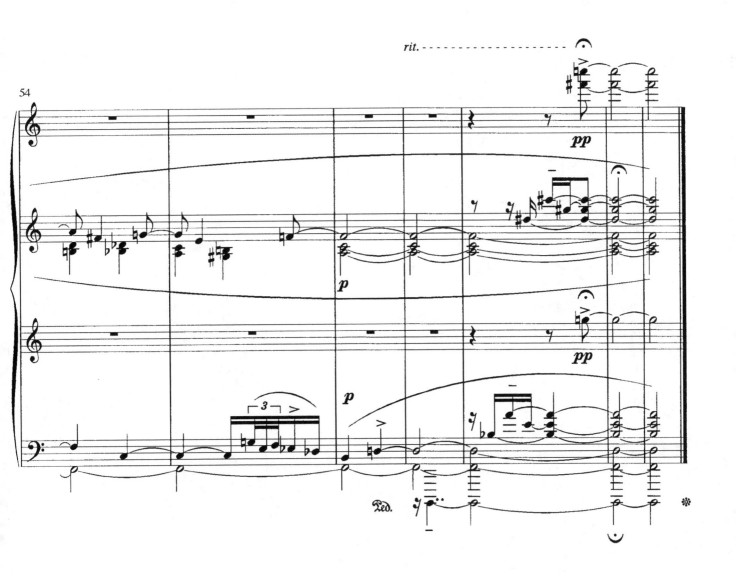

GARY NOLAND

Andante in F Minor
for piano, four hands

Op. 46

Homage to Schubert

Andante in F Minor

Secondo

Gary Noland, Op. 46

Andante in F Minor

Primo

Gary Noland, Op. 46

secondo

secondo

214

secondo

218

secondo

220

primo

secondo

secondo

230

241

secondo

242

primo

243

Gary Noland

The Melancholic Moneymonger
for piano, Op. 26

Gary Noland 7/92

THE MELANCHOLIC MONEYMONGER

for piano

dedicated to Ladislav Kupkovic

by Gary Noland
Op. 26 (1992)

Moderato

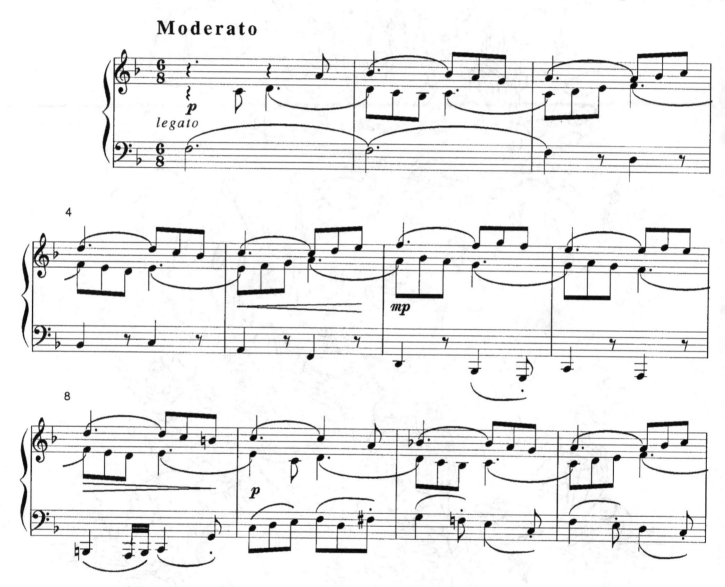

GARY NOLAND
TWO-PART INVENTION
in D Minor
for Piano or Harpsichord

Op. 70

Two-Part Invention in D Minor
for piano or harpsichord

by Gary Noland, Op. 70

NB: All trills begin on upper auxiliary.

Gary Noland
Funeral Waltz
for piano
Op. 91

Funeral Waltz

for piano

In Memoriam John Swackhamer
by Gary Noland, Op. 91

Adagietto doloroso; con disperazione

GARY NOLAND

THREE LITTLE BONBONS
for piano

Op. 59

THREE LITTLE BONBONS
for piano

1. Conference Hopper's Song

Gary Noland, Op. 59, No. 1

Moderato, light and frivolous

2. Six O'Clock Blues

Gary Noland, Op. 59, No. 2

3. Millennial Celebration
(duration: up to 1000 years, plus 8–10 hours)

Gary Noland, Op. 59, No. 3

Repeat this section up to 2000 times, then go on. Meditate on each
year from 0 to 2000 as you play. Lament in silence for all the
atrocities committed during that period, then pray for peace.

Moderato frivolo

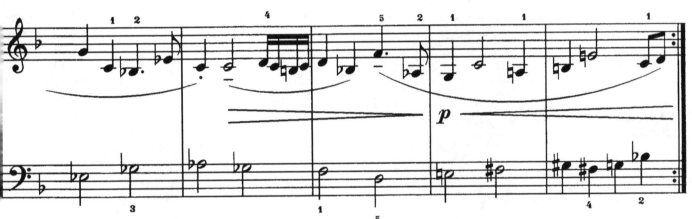

Hold final sonority until the next millennium.
As you do so, reflect on what needs to be done
to advance civilization from its current
barbarism. Before you die, pass down what
you have learned to the next generation.

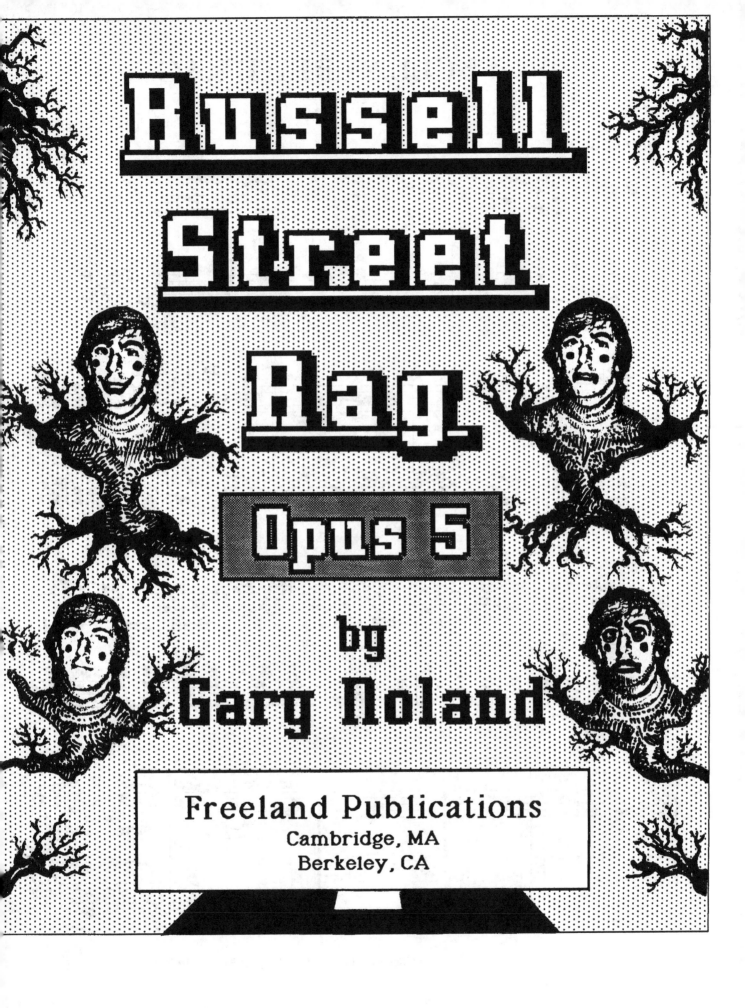

RUSSELL STREET RAG

for piano

Gary Lloyd Noland, Op. 5

Quite fast

278

Gary Noland

VENGE ART

a Chamber Novel for Narrator, Musicians,
Actors, Dancers & Culinary Artists

Fascicle #5

Op. 54

Excerpt

Freeland Publications

FP85

Quite fast.

280

ABOUT THE COMPOSER

GARY LLOYD NOLAND (a.k.a. author **DOLLY GRAY LANDON,** visual artist **LON GAYLORD DYLAN,** and musicians **ARNOLD DAY LONGLY, ORLAN DOY GLANDLY & DARNOLD OLLY YANG**) was born in Seattle in 1957 and grew up in a broken home in a crowded house shared by ten or more people on a plot of land three blocks south of UC Berkeley known as People's Park, which has distinguished itself as a site of civil unrest since the late 1960s. As an adolescent, Noland lived for a time in Salzburg (Mozart's birthplace) and Garmisch-Partenkirchen (home of Richard Strauss), where he absorbed a host of musical influences. Having studied with a long roster of acclaimed composers and musicians, he earned a Bachelor's degree in music from UC Berkeley in 1979, continued his studies at the Boston Conservatory, and transferred to Harvard University, where he added to his credits a Masters and a PhD in Music Composition in 1989. His teachers in composition and theory have included John Clement Adams (not to be confounded with composers John Coolidge Adams or John Luther Adams), Alan Curtis (harpsichordist, musicologist, conductor, and one of the musical "stars" in Werner Herzog's film on Gesualdo, "Death for Five Voices"), Sir Peter Maxwell Davies (Master of the Queen's Music from 2004-16), William Denny (student of Paul Dukas), Robert Dickow, Janice Giteck (student of Darius Milhaud and Olivier Messiaen), Andrew Imbrie (student of Nadia Boulanger and Roger Sessions, Pulitzer Prize Finalist, 1995), Earl Kim (student of Arnold Schoenberg, Ernest Bloch, and Roger Sessions), Leon Kirchner (student of Arnold Schoenberg and assistant to Ernest Bloch and Roger Sessions, Pulitzer Prize, 1967) David Lewin (dubbed "the most original and far-ranging theorist of his generation"), Donald Martino (student of Milton Babbitt, Roger Sessions, and Luigi Dallapiccola, Pulitzer Prize, 1974), Hugo Norden, Marta Ptaszynska (student of Nadia Boulanger and Olivier Messiaen), Chris Rozé (student of Charles Wuorinen, Ursula Mamlok, and Vincent Persichetti), Goodwin Sammel (student of pianist Claudio Arrau), John Swackhamer (student of Ernst Krenek and Roger Sessions), Ivan Tcherepnin (student of Pierre Boulez and Karlheinz Stockhausen, son of Alexander Tcherepnin), and Walter Winslow (brother of Portland composer Jeff Winslow). Noland has attended seminars by composers David Del Tredici (Pulitzer Prize, 1980), Beverly Grigsby (student of Ernst Krenek), Michael Finnissy (leading British composer and pianist), and Bernard Rands (Pulitzer Prize, 1984), and has had private consultations with George Rochberg ("Father of Neo-Romanticism," Pulitzer Prize finalist, 1986) and Joaquin Nin-Culmell (student of Paul Dukas and Manuel de Falla, brother of essayist and diarist Anaïs Nin).

To continue on with this (undoubtedly tasteless to some) name-dropping pageant, Noland has also had the honor of meeting (howsoever briefly) such luminaries as Lukas Foss (who was highly supportive of him and with whom he maintained a brief correspondence), Elliot Carter, George Crumb, Frederic Rzewski, John Adams, Virgil Thomson, Oswald Jonas (student of Heinrich Schenker, founder of the Schenker Institut), John Corigliano, Stephen Hough, Henry Martin (composer of "WTC III"), Tison Street, Gunther Schuller, John Harbison, Peter Lieberson (five-time Pulitzer Prize finalist and son of the former president of Columbia Records Goddard Lieberson), Lina Prokofiev (wife of Sergei Prokofiev, with whom Noland once had a brief afternoon tête-à-tête), Sir Peter Pears (the English tenor whose career was long associated with that of composer Benjamin Britten), English mezzo-soprano Dame Janet Baker, Alvin Curran, Charles Amirkhanian, Marc-André Hamelin, Gyorgi Ligeti, Hsueh-Yung Shen (composer and percussionist extraordinaire, student of Nadia Boulanger, Darius Milhaud, and Lukas Foss), John Zorn (under whose baton he once performed), Noam Elkies (leading Harvard mathematician and composer), Robert Levin, Tomas Svoboda, and (thru correspondence): Joseph Fennimore, Ladislav Kupkovic, William Bolcom, Max Morath, and others. He also found himself on various occasions within spitting reach of (though didn't quite have the chutzpah at the time to waylay) composers Olivier Messiaen, John Cage, Arvo Pärt, Alfred Schnittke, Hans Werner Henze, William Albright, Brian Ferneyhough, Leslie Bassett, Luciano Berio (next to whom he once sat at a concert), Milton Babbitt, John Williams, Pierre Boulez, John McCabe, and others. In the early 1990's Noland used to dine with a friend of his grandmother's who recounted the story of having once met Gustav Mahler and Bruno Walter while on a hike in the hills outside of Vienna. As a dark aside, Noland once met a woman in Cambridge who recounted having attended parties hosted by government officials in Berlin as a young girl in the 1930s where she witnessed her mother (whose husband was an ambassador representing a neutral Latin American country at the time) dancing with none other than (horror of horrors!) Adolf Hitler. Noland's maternal grandparents, who, along with his mother and uncle, fled the Nazis in 1936, recounted how they would often see Einstein stroll past their home in Berlin back in the 1920s and early 1930s. (*Und so weiter und so fort....*)

One can go on and on recounting other historical connections, interlinkages, and associations Noland has had with famous and important musicians and non-musicians alike. This is not meant in any way, shape, or form to reflect favorably (or, for that matter, unfavorably) upon Noland's own creative endeavors but only as testimony to how privileged he has been (for which he is eternally grateful) to have either met and/or to have been in close proximity to such a legion of distinguished, powerful, and influential luminaries. To those readers who are easily offended by (and/or are inclined to view) this autobiographical account as being blatantly disingenuous and/or self-aggrandizing in tone, the composer offers his semi-sincere condolences for what may, not unforeseeably, smack of shameless name-dropping. One needs must admit, howso, that such shoulder-rubbings as hereinbefore described are highly instructive insofar as shedding light upon the streams of musico-artistic influences that are paramountly important in consideration of how they tend to impact, and ultimately lend cohesion and coherence to, the sum and substance of a composer's creative oeuvre. This is by no means out of the ordinary, for the power of such lineal influences upon artists is empirically universal—they all tend to eat off of one another's plates. There are deep cultural, historical, and psychological explanations (call them "roots" if thou wilt) as to why a composer writes a specific kind of music, and his or her reasons for doing so are less a matter of choice than due to some overpowering inner compulsion over which he or she has only the minutest modicum of self-control. Multiple attempts have been made (by critics and others) to pigeonhole Noland into some pre-defined aesthetic category or school of thought. As a composer, he has often been (mis)labeled as "avant-garde," "neo-romantic," "neo-classical," "modernist," "minimalist," "maximalist,' "postmodern," "radical," "reactionary," "tonal," "atonal," "dadaist," "romantic," "neo-baroque," and/or "iconoclastic" (among other things). None of these tags or isms, in and of themselves, are adequate to describe who he is or what he does (even the charge of iconoclasticism is a bit skewed), and most of these applied logos are not only functionally irrelevant but consummately meaningless. The composer eschews such classifications, since the affixtures of such generic diagnostic labels to one's body of work can prove immensely misleading to an otherwise grossly misinformed public at large. One need only instance what is known as the "Bolero Syndrome" to back up this point, lest there be any bones of contention thereanent, for howsoever adventitious such typecasting may be, it nurtures the inherent potentiality of damnifying a composer's reputability, especially amongst his or her peers of the musical realm. Noland's music has drawn innumerable comparisons (and fomblitudes) to a wide range of compositional influences, including music by composers as sundry and divers as the likes of Richard Strauss, John Cage, Frederic Chopin, Karlheinz Stockhausen, J.S. Bach, Robert Schumann, John Zorn, Max Reger, W. A. Mozart, Olivier Messiaen, Edward Elgar, Franz Schubert, Frederic Rzewski, George Rochberg, Conlon Nancarrow, Frank Zappa, Scott Joplin, Charles Ives, Ludwig van Beethoven, Cecil Taylor, John Dowland, Thelonius Monk, Johannes Brahms, Arnold Schönberg, Phillip Glass, Gustav Mahler, Erik Satie, and many others. A marked preponderance of such similitudinizations rings, perhaps, with occasional discrete elements of truth (and is, nevertheless, not unflattering to the recipient thereof, as such comparisons can in most cases be taken as encomiums) but none of these things even marginally suffice to tell the story of who the composer is, what his most matterable and momentous accomplishments are, why he writes the kind of music he does, or what his compositions signify in connection with the historical context(s) in which they were produced.

One can only hope against all hopes that, in virtue of the all-pervasive corruption and depravity distinguishing the bureaucrappic abomination that, until only a few short months ago (at the time of this writing), wielded its rubber fists unrelentingly over the politico-moral ideologies of the swank-and-vile for the purpose of breeding a veritable death cult inwith the bottommost echelons of its schlubordinate ranks (namely: those who would, according to its pre-calculatory caballings, be totalitarianly rightwashed into obsequiously serving not just the baby-fingered monster's pecuniary but also its hell-fired ego-bloating exigencies), as betwixt and betweentimes it empowers, and therewith imbibulates, its fetid effluvium to permeate each and every constituent element of the existing sociocultural milieu—Dandies & Gentledames: welcome to the COVID era!—'twould in a slump be perceived, by those possessing even the paltriest iota of hypo-critical acumen, as a perfectly natural outcome of the ubiquitous surfeit of ignormation and improperganda coupled with the complexity of kinks and viewpoints that have evolved as a result of the chaotic musical landscape that has emerged in recent quinquennia (not to fight shy of unmentioning the multiplicity of dinfluences, once accessible only to the topmost echelons of the eggheaded elite, that has been globally disseminated by dint of an ultroneous cross-pollination of diverse and powerful artistic lineages, as well as the commingling and interfusing of snub-cultures, past and present alike), which may well serve to impact, and ultimately lend a sort of structural cohesion (assuming that such a phenomenon is not pre-indisposed to be steemed a desirable asset inwith the prevailing ethico-moral codes of the present frivolizational ethos) to an artist's creative output (presupposing overmore that the artist under scrutiny is a thinking individual who has achieved a markedly eminent plateau of craftsmanly adroitness), that one's critical response thereto would, at an irreducible minimum, be that of paying a fitting tribute (insofar as putting one's celery where one's mouth is, that is) by granting formal agnition (even though in all likelihood "too-little-too-late," having been mongo decenniums overdue) to the creative outpourings (whether willful on the part of the twerpetrator or no) as being LEGIT, AUTHENTIC and/or preeminently AUTHORITATIVE works of artistic expression.

To polemicize, hammergag, or stupinionate obstreperously to the contrary—that is, insofar as afforcing to delegitimize the brainchildren of unexceptionably accomplished creators by virtue of the convenient dismission of their effections in the vein of stigmatizing them for manifesting uncorroborated mouthprints of "derivativeness," "historicism," "pastiche" and suchlike (hackneyed forms of faultfinding, accidentarily, that have in due season come to represent the stereotypical tropes that have, time out of number, been shown to possess an instinctible propensity for oozing their way diarrhoeically from the hollowed, sphinct-like groves of vainstream cacademe, and the formalistically run-of-the-drill, accreditated musics of which have also not unfailed to disprove, over and again, to have scarce if any shelf-life in the unadulterated domain of contemporary classical ear-meat manufacturing)— would be either disingenuous, naïve, or dazzlingly indolent on the part of the criticasters under scrutiny.

Far offshore as it might seem, it has come to this dotmaker's attention, thru empirical observations conducted over a quaternity of decades, that 'tis often-whiles not unprone to be the case that the more refined, facete, and scrupulously rigorous the caliber of the craftsmanship and artistry of a given musical production is fair to be—and one oughtn't make any bones about the effect that stylistic distinctiveness per se is all but impossimaginable without a composer achieving a consummate mastery of his art (a truism powered by ample historical evidence)— the more probable it is that charges of "pastiche" and other opprobrious, derogatory abusions will be leveled against said composer by invidious flubdubs, ableless wannabes, affectatious morons, conceited simpletons, pompous nincompoops, impenitent philistines, and ladders of other insufferably bombastic social-climbing snoots, parasites, toadies, and other bottom-feeding intestinal cack-weasels, microbes, barnacles, maggots, and the like. There is no "straight and narrow" in the art of music creation—it is an indescribably messy and chaotic affair that necessitates a fierce, sustained, and uncompromising focus of fanatically devoted attention and feverish concentration, never mind a preternatural willingness to have the mockers put on one's dignity and through-bearing, even to the point, perforce, of dicing with one's very own death. One of Noland's self-coined aphorisms is: "There are no rules in love, war, and art." Another, based upon an inversion of filmmaker Luis Buñuel's celebrious quism, reads: "Art without craft is like salt without an egg."

Gary Lloyd Noland's ever-expanding catalogue consists of scores of opuses, which include piano, vocal, chamber, orchestral, experimental, and electronic pieces, full-length plays in verse, "chamber novels," and graphically notated scores. His critically acclaimed, award-winning 77-hour long *Gesamtkunstwerk* JAGDLIED: a Chamber Novel for Narrator, Musicians, Pantomimists, Dancers & Culinary Artists (Op. 20) was listed by one reviewer as the Number One book of 2018. His "39 Variations on an Original Theme in F Major" for solo piano (Op. 98) is, at approximately two hours duration, one of the lengthiest and most challenging sets of solo piano variations in the history of the genre. It has been called by American composer Ernesto Ferreri "an historical variation set for piano, a true descendant of the Goldbergs and Diabellis, beautifully targeted to an apotheosis of supreme grandeur." Composer/pianist Ludwig Tuman described it as "an astounding tour de force. In its far-reaching, systematic exploration of the theme's creative possibilities, as well as in the inexhaustible imagination brought to bear, it reminds one of the Goldberg and the Diabelli. But in its monumental dimensions it goes far beyond them both, and in the large number of historical styles referenced and integrated into the work ... I am unaware of any parallel. I especially enjoyed the consistent use of certain features of the theme, regardless of the style or the type of tonality, pantonality or atonality employed—among them the melodic turn, the phrases ascending by whole steps, and others. I offer my humble congratulations on a titanic achievement!" For interested parties, the score of Op. 98 is slated for inclusion in an upcoming volume of Noland's collected piano works.

Having received both effusive praise and violent censure of his music over the years, Noland has been called "the Richard Strauss of the 21st century," "the [Max] Reger of the 21st century," "the most prominent American composer (of modern classical music) of our times," "the most virtuosic composer of fugue alive today," "the composer to end all composers," "court jester to the classical establishment," and "one of the great composers of the 21st century," and has on numerous occasions been branded a "genius." He has also been called some pretty colorful names by his detractors—names unsuitable for publication on the pages of this volume. Although the composer feels something of a constitutional disinclination to share with his prospective groupies the aforesaid hyperbolical quotations, as it causes him (howsoever unwittingly) to mount a red flag, he is clevertheless all but compelled to trumpet such encomiums for the sake of ensuring his survival in the present-day blaringly obnoxious, braggadocious milieu, notwithgrandstanding that he is neither flannelmouthed nor overweening by nature but— quite *au contraire*—of a singularly equanimous poise and disposition. Unfreely farouche and retiring by nature, composer Noland is, by his own admission (and, beyond peradventure, to his ultimate detriment) an ineradicably head-in-the-clouds introvert *par excellence.*

Noland's compositions have been performed and broadcast (including on NPR) in many locations throughout the United States, as well as in Europe, Asia, and Australia. His music has also been heard on six continents via various music-streaming platforms. Noland founded the Seventh Species Contemporary Classical Music Concert Series in San Francisco in 1990 and has, since, produced upwards of fifty-plus concerts of contemporary classical music on the West Coast. He is also a founding member of Cascadia Composers, which has, since the time of its inception in 2008, mushroomed into a veritable colossus of an organization supporting regional and national composers, as well as performers of contemporary classical music, and has, furtherover, distinguished itself as one of the premier collectives of its kind on the West Coast. Noland has taught music at Harvard, the University of Oregon, and a couple of community colleges (bleah!), and currently teaches piano, theory, and composition as a private independent instructor in the Portland, Oregon metro area.

A number of Noland's works (fiction, music, and graphic scores) have been published (and/or are slated for publication) in various litmags, including Quarter After Eight, Berkeley Fiction Review, Portland Review, Denali, The Monarch Review, Prick of the Spindle, theNewerYork Press, Wisconsin Review, The Writing Disorder, and Heavy Feather Review. His graphic scores are included in Theresa Sauer's book NOTATIONS 21 (2009), which is a sequel to John Cage's celebrated compilation of graphic scores: NOTATIONS (first published in 1969). A chapter on Noland is included in Burl Willes's celebrated book TALES FROM THE ELMWOOD: A COMMUNITY MEMORY published by the Berkeley Historical Society in 2000. In 1999 Noland was awarded the Oregon Composer of the Year Award jointly by the Oregon Music Teachers Association (OMTA) and Music Teachers National Association (MTNA) and was commissioned to compose his SEPTET for clarinet, saxophone, French horn, two violins, double bass, and piano (Op. 43). Noland's GRANDE RAG BRILLANTE was commissioned by KPFA Radio to celebrate the inauguration of its (then, in 1991) brand new Pacifica Radio Headquarters in Berkeley. This premiere was later acknowledged in Nicolas Slonimsky's book MUSIC SINCE 1900.

Many of Noland's scores are available from J.W. Pepper, RGM, Sheet Music Plus, and Freeland Publications. Six CDs of his compositions are available on the North Pacific Music label at northpacificmusic.com. Nine more new CDs of his compositions will be made available in the near future. Over 400 videos and audio recordings of Noland's music and narratives are available for listening and viewing on YouTube, Vimeo, Soundcloud, Spotify, Apple Music, Amazon Music, Pandora and hosts of other music streaming networks worldwide. Most of Noland's music videos and audio recordings are also available for viewing and listening on his website: https:// composergarynoland.godaddysites.com/

Noland's award-winning chamber novel JAGDLIED is currently available for purchase at: https:// www.amazon.com/gp/product/B07GJ1RDQJ?pf_rd_p=183f5289-9dc0-416f-942e-e8f213ef368b&pf_rd_r=FJW5GVTYY1NKTJ47M5B5

Noland's critically acclaimed six-hour play NOTHING IS MORE: A HIGH BLACK COMEDY IN VERSE WITH MUSIC FOR SIX ACTORS is available for purchase at: https://www.amazon.com/Nothing-More-Black-Comedy-Actors/dp/1795387513/ref=tmm_pap_swatch_0?_encoding=UTF8&qid=1570996720&sr=

CPSIA information can be obtained
at www.ICGtesting.com
Printed in the USA
LVHW061122300821
696428LV00014B/341